Chinese Painting and Calligraphy

Marie Morrison

CRAZY COOL CHINA

ROSEN PUBLISHING
NEW YORK

SinolinguA
华语教学出版社
BEIJING

Published in 2025 by The Rosen Publishing Group, Inc.
29 East 21st Street, New York, NY 10010

Jointly published in 2025 by Sinolingua Co.,Ltd., Beijing, China, and The Rosen Publishing Group, Inc., New York, New York, United States.

First Edition

Editor: Marie Morrison
Designer: Rachel Rising

Photo credits: Cover BinGoTinGo/Shutterstock.com; pp. 1, 3-48 Sylfida/Shutterstock.com; pp. 4,6, 10, 14, 18, 22, 26, 30, 34, 38, 42 vetre/Shutterstock.com; p. 5 Nor Gal/Shutterstock.com; p. 7 Tatiana_kashko_photo/Shutterstock.com; p. 8 https://en.m.wikipedia.org/wiki/File:Admonitions_Scroll_Scene_4_(Song_copy).jpg; p.11 https://en.m.wikipedia.org/wiki/File:Night_Shining_White; p. 12 zhaoliang70/Shutterstock.com; p.15 Giusparta/Shutterstock.com; p.16 https://commons.wikimedia.org/wiki/File:Guo_Xi_-_Early_Spring_(large).jpg; p. 17 DreamArchitect/Shutterstock.com; p. 19 Joinmepic/Shutterstock.com;
p.20 https://commons.wikimedia.org/wiki/File:Xu_Wei.JPG; p. 20 https://en.m.wikipedia.org/wiki/File:Chrysanthemums_and_Bamboos_by_Xu_Wei.jpg; p. 23 https://en.m.wikipedia.org/wiki/File:Ren_Bonian_-_Playing_the_Flute_-_Walters_35101C.jpg; 24 https://commons.wikimedia.org/wiki/File:Elegance_of_Lotus_Looking_from_Heaven.jpg; p. 25 https://commons.wikimedia.org/wiki/Category:Paintings_of_horses_by_Xu_Beihong; p. 27 toonman/Shutterstock.com; p. 28 Sun Xuejun/Shutterstock.com; p.31 Horydczak, Theodor, Approximately, photographer. Library of Congress John Adams Building. Figure of Ts'ang Chieh on door, Library of Congress annex. ca. 1920-ca. 1950. Photograph. Retrieved from the Library of Congress, <www.loc.gov/item/2019682834/>.; p.32 https://zh.wikipedia.org/wiki/File:8_strokes_of_%E6%B0%B8-zh.svg; p. 35 https://commons.wikimedia.org/wiki/File:Portraits_of_Famous_Men_-_Wang_Xizhi.jpg; p. 35 https://en.m.wikipedia.org/wiki/File:LantingXu.jpg; p. 36 Xinhua / Alamy Stock Photo; p. 36 Xinhua / Alamy Stock Photo;
p. 39 danielcastromaia/Shutterstock.com; p. 40 Mirko Kuzmanovic/Shutterstock.com; p. 43 WaitForLight/Shutterstock.com.

Cataloging-in-Publication Data
Names: Morrison, Marie.
Title: Chinese painting and calligraphy / Marie Morrison.
Description: Buffalo, NY : Rosen Young Adult, 2025. | Series: Crazy cool China |
Includes glossary and index.
Identifiers: ISBN 9781499476187 (pbk.) | ISBN 9781499476194 (library bound) |
ISBN 9781499476200 (ebook)
Subjects: LCSH: Painting, Chinese–Technique.| Ink painting, Chinese–Technique. |
Calligraphy, Chinese. | Calligraphy, Chinese–Technique.
Classification: LCC ND1040.M856 2025 | DDC 759.951-dc23

Manufactured in the United States of America

CPSIA Compliance Information: Batch #CSRYA25. For further information, contact Rosen Publishing at 1-800-237-9932.

Contents

The Art of the Line

China, both in ancient times and modern society, has many forms of thriving art. In fact, the nation has the oldest continuous **tradition** of art in the world. However, perhaps the most well known are two **intricately** linked art forms: painting and calligraphy. Both have a long, vivid history in the region, and both have many noted practitioners throughout the ages. Both have a strong and storied link to Chinese culture and history.

Traditional Chinese noble **scholars** were expected to master four arts: calligraphy, painting, playing the percussion instrument called the *qin*, and playing the board game Go. While this book focuses on the first two, the latter two skills also go back thousands of years in Chinese culture.

Calligraphy has been called the art of the line. The word refers to the practice of creating artistic writing or lettering, often with the characters shaped in a stylized fashion. One doesn't need to be able to read or write

Chinese characters to appreciate the graceful lines of Chinese calligraphy. It's so predominant among the traditional art forms of China that Chinese painting tends to be judged by the same standards as its calligraphy: the expressiveness of the lines and the harmony of the piece as a whole.

People often consider calligraphy and painting the foremost of China's traditional arts.

Ancient Art

The history of Chinese art is about as long as Chinese history itself. Early humans created paintings on pottery, an art that dates back more than 10,000 years in the region. The Yangshao culture of **Neolithic** China is even called the "painted pottery" culture. Their pottery was decorated with designs in colors that included white, red, and black.

The creation of silk fabric is a major art of China itself. The earliest example of this fabric was found in Henan Province in China and dates to 3630 BCE. Artists would use a stone to smooth the silk and then paint it with designs or works of calligraphy.

People also created paintings on cliffs and cave walls throughout the region. Some well-known examples of these cliff paintings are in Zuojiang Huashan Rock Art Cultural Landscape in southwest China. These date to about the fifth century BCE. Soon after, before paper was invented about 100 BCE, people developed the art of silk painting. The earliest forms of this art date to about 476 BCE.

This artwork is from the Zuojiang Huashan Rock Art Cultural Landscape in Guangxi, China. It's a **UNESCO** World **Heritage** site.

This portion of a copy of *The Admonitions of the Instructress to the Court Ladies* is in the Palace Museum in Beijing.

Gu Kaizhi wrote books on painting theory, or the general ideas that have to do with painting. These books include *On Painting, Introduction of Famous Paintings of Wei and Jin Dynasties*, and *Painting Yuntai Mountain*. He also wrote many poems and essays.

The time of the Han **Dynasty** is sometimes called the golden age of Chinese art. This period stretched from 206 BCE to 220 CE and included the rise of many art forms, including music, dance, architecture, painting, and sculpture. About a century later, about 340 CE, a man who'd be called "the founder of Chinese painting" was born. Gu Kaizhi was a poet, writer, politician, and painter from Wuxi, China.

Paper had been invented by this time, but the examples of Gu Kaizhi's work that survive are on silk scrolls. Perhaps the best known is *Nymph of the Luo River*. Several copies of this work can still be seen today. It illustrates a poem written in 222 CE. Another work is *The Admonitions of the Instructress to the Court Ladies*.

Figure and Landscape Painting

China's Tang Dynasty arose about 618 CE (after the Sui Dynasty) and was a flourishing era for art and culture. Figure painting was popular at the royal court. Historians know the names of more artists from this period. Notable names include Yan Liben, Zhou Fang, and Zhang Xuan.

One particularly well-known painter was Wu Daozi, who lived in the 700s. There are many stories about him, so many that it can be hard to separate **legend** from fact. He painted many **murals**, but most, if not all, of his works do not survive. Wu Daozi

Horses, of great importance during the Tang Dynasty, were popular subjects for painting. Painter Han Gan was known for his images of the animals, said to capture their spirit as well as their likeness. Another artist known for the subject was Cao Ba, a general.

was considered a master of brushwork who only used black ink. Stories say that crowds would gather to watch him paint.

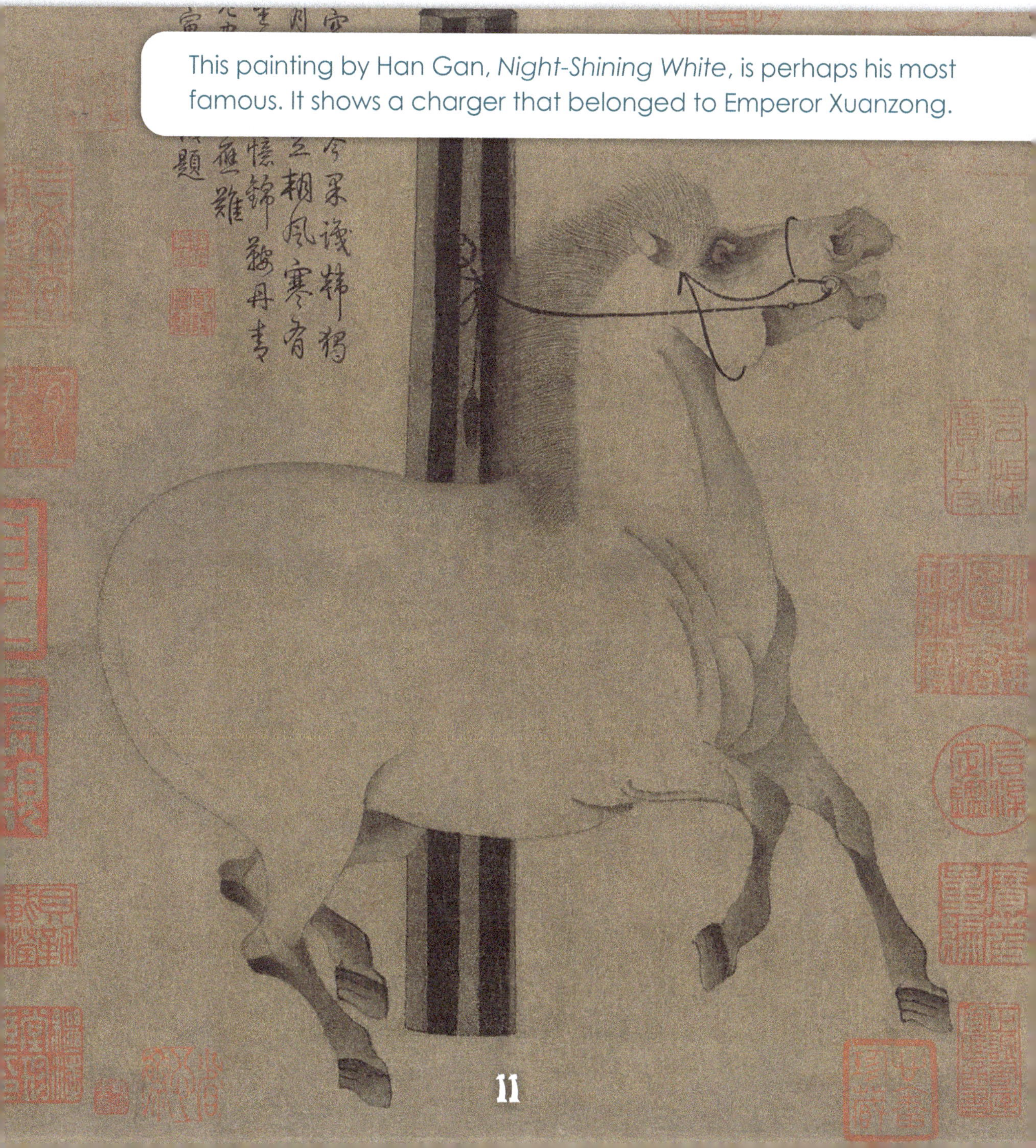

This painting by Han Gan, *Night-Shining White*, is perhaps his most famous. It shows a charger that belonged to Emperor Xuanzong.

This statue shows poet and painter Wang Wei. He founded what's called the "Southern school" of painter-poets.

Another very old Chinese art form is lacquerware. These objects are covered with lacquer, which is a hard, usually shiny, coating. They're often painted with pictures as well. Many beautiful lacquerware objects, including musical instruments, remain from the Tang Dynasty.

As the Tang Dynasty continued, landscape painting developed a great deal. Different styles focus on different colors and **techniques**. *Shanshui* (mountain-water) is a type of traditional landscape painting. *Jinbi shanshui* is a style that uses blue, green, and gold. Painter Li Sixun and his son Li Zhaodao particularly made use of these styles and are among the most famous artists of the time.

Poet and scholar Wang Wei lived during the eighth century. Some say he founded the school of scholarly landscape painting called *wenrenhua*. The scholar-painters, also trained in calligraphy, focused on expressing themselves more than reproducing actual images. Many of Wang Wei's poems were inspired by landscapes, and many of those still survive.

Great Rival Artists

The Tang Dynasty fell about 907. It was followed by the Five Dynasties period, which lasted until about 960. One notable landscape painter during this time was Jing Hao. Two paintings credited to him are *Mount Kuanglu and Travelers in a Snowy Landscape.* He created a new style of landscape painting, with bold images of mountains and other landforms in ink.

After the Five Dynasties, the Northern Song Dynasty arose. These were important times in Chinese landscape painting. Historians know of many artists, and somewhat more work survives. Other arts, such as pottery and carving, were also popular. A few notable painters of this time were sometimes called the three great rival artists. These were Li Cheng, Fan Kuan, and Guan Tong.

> Huizong was one of the last emperors of the Northern Song Dynasty. He offered much support to the arts and was himself a painter and calligrapher. However, while he focused on the arts, the downfall of the Dynasty began. His son Qinzong was the final Northern Song emperor.

Tall pagodas such as the one shown here were noted parts of Song Dynasty architecture.

Early Spring is probably Guo Xi's most well-known work. It shows many of the notable techniques he used.

The Northern Song Dynasty was followed by the Southern Song. It was called so because the Dynasty had lost control of the north and had to move to the south of China. Figure painting again became more prominent at court during this time.

Guan Tong was a follower of Jing Hao, and Li Cheng was, in turn, a follower of Guan Tong. The three great rival artists don't have much (if any) surviving artworks. We know them through copies and their **influence** on later artists. Like Jing Hao before them, they tended to use strong, crisp dark lines, washes of ink, and dotted brushwork.

Guo Xi was one **prominent** landscape painter who followed the three rivals in the Northern Song. His notes on painting, called *Linquan Gaozhi*, or *Lofty Message of Forests and Streams*, include much information on techniques and the **philosophy** of painting. Some of the paintings attributed to him are *Early Spring* (1072) and *The Coming of Autumn*.

Guo Xi was from Henan Province. The region has a very long history.

Masters and Dynasties

After the end of the Song Dynasty in the 13th century, **Mongols** took control of part and then all of China. This was the time of the Yuan Dynasty. Artistically speaking, this time is known for the so-called Four Great Masters: Huang Gongwang, Ni Zan, Wu Zhen, and Wang Meng. These artists all excelled at landscape painting. Still, all had styles that were very much their own.

Before the Four Great Masters, there was Zhao Mengfu. In 1286, this great painter and calligrapher accepted service in the Mongol imperial court. Many artists of the time preferred to withdraw and avoid serving the Mongols, and Zhao Mengfu was sometimes **criticized** for this choice. He was known for his paintings of horses, other animals, and landscapes.

The Four Great Masters were part of the earlier mentioned tradition of *wenrenhua*, or scholarly painting. This tradition continued to be about expression more than visuals. With these masters, landscape painting focused more on capturing the idea of nature rather than exactly reproducing it.

This Chinese stamp shows the painting *Bathing Horses* by Zhao Mengfu. His wife and son were also skilled painters.

Xu Wei was also a poet and a tea master. He led an often chaotic life, and his works often seem to reflect a great deal of emotion.

Both the Qing orthodox painters and the individualists followed the theories of Dong Qichang, a painter and calligrapher of the late Ming Dynasty. His ideas still influence some Chinese art today. He wrote a lot about painting, calligraphy, and their traditions in Chinese art.

With the rise of the Ming Dynasty in 1368, Chinese arts, including painting, entered a new golden age, and calligraphy became even more involved in painting. The two contrasting schools of painting were the Wu school and the Zhe school. Some of the prominent painters of the time included Bian Wenjin, Lu Ji, Dai Jin, Shen Zhou, Wen Zhengming, and Xu Wei.

The Ming Dynasty was followed in 1644 by the Qing Dynasty, the last dynasty of imperial China. This span of years included the orthodox painters and the individualists, who both had different approaches to art. The individualists tended to push back against the traditional rules and focused on self-expression. Toward the end of the dynasty's time, more Western influence slowly entered Chinese art. Some artists worked to combine both traditions.

Modern Times

In 1911 and 1912, many changes and a **revolution** brought about the downfall of China's dynastic system. The Republic of China was founded in 1911. In a relatively quick fashion, many other changes also took place: The War of Resistance Against Japanese Aggression from 1931 to 1945, a civil war, and the founding of the People's Republic of China in 1949. Each shift brought corresponding changes in Chinese painting styles and artistic schools.

Oil painting as an art form came to China in the 1600s, but it truly became popular in the 20th century, especially in the 1980s. The medium was a distinct departure from the ink paintings of earlier times, but many artists still created traditional scenes as in earlier works. Artist Jin Shangyi of Beijing is one notable Chinese oil painter.

After the earlier part of the 1900s, more young Chinese artists studied art in Japan, Germany, France, and other regions, bringing aspects of new traditions and art movements home. The city of Shanghai became a noted arts center in the 20th

Today, Shanghai is a major industrial center of China and a large seaport. It has more people than any other city in China.

Artist Ren Yi, born in 1840, was a painter of the Shanghai School. This work is called *Playing the Flute*.

century, and a distinct Shanghai style of art arose. It was inspired by individualist artists, using traditional styles in new ways. Art also gained a more public audience.

Since the reform and opening up in the late 1970s, artists started working in newer experimental ways while also bringing about a return of traditional painting. Over the past 40 years or so, artists have continued to work with new techniques, styles, and subjects, with many still striving for more freedom of expression.

Chinese artist Shaoqiang Chen, who was born in 1981, is known as the creator of Heaven Style painting. This style combines some classic styles from imperial China with some Western techniques, often with an overhead view. One well-known piece of his is *Elegance of the Lotus Looking from Heaven*.

Xu Beihong was a Chinese painter of the 20th century. He was known for his paintings of birds and horses and is considered a pioneer of Chinese modern art. This stamp shows some of his work.

Calligraphy Connections

Chinese calligraphy is, as noted earlier, closely tied to traditional painting. It's the writing of Chinese characters as a form of art. People speak many **dialects** in China, and these are often not mutually understandable. Calligraphy connects them. In this art form, the characters can stand for the idea of their subject rather than simply its name. How someone writes can be just as important (or more important) than what someone writes.

The practice of calligraphy has led to other forms of art in China. The tools traditionally used to create calligraphy are a brush, ink, an ink stone (used with water to make ink), and paper (or silk). Making these items can also be art, and they're collectively called the Four Treasures of the Study.

The artist brings both skill and creativity to the art, shaping the lines in an attractive and graceful way while balancing the spaces between the brushstrokes. This can include carefully controlling the brush in its direction, pressure, and speed. It takes a lot of practice to do this well. Many aspects of the calligraphy tools, such as the makeup of the brush and the ink, can also make a big difference in the finished piece.

There can be many variations in the traditional tools used for calligraphy. A brush can have a body made of various materials and a head made from various types of hair.

The different Chinese languages are often called dialects, but they are different languages in the same family. They include Mandarin, Wu, Northern and Southern Min, Gan, Hakka, Xiang, and Cantonese. Mandarin is the most widely spoken. More people speak a Chinese language as a native speaker than any other form of language in the world.

The origins of Chinese characters can be traced back more than 3,000 years. In fact, many historians think that China is one of only four places around the world where writing developed independently. (The others are Mesopotamia, Egypt, and Mesoamerica.) Chinese characters and words are still more linked to the image they represent than is the case with Western alphabets and words, though they have evolved considerably over time.

The oldest existing examples of Chinese calligraphy are carved on animal bones and turtle shells and date to about 2000 BCE. It can still be readable today. However, because of the different instruments used to create it, the strokes used are far more abrupt.

The oldest known Chinese writing is in oracle bone **script**, such as the calligraphy shown engraved here.

Through the Years

While the earliest Chinese calligraphy was engraved, the tools used today are still tightly linked to its history. Calligraphers do sometimes use silk, but the invention of paper (done first in China) in the first century CE brought about many new possibilities. Starting during the Han Dynasty (206 BCE to 220 CE) in China, calligraphers began to use brushes consistently for their art.

Legends say that a historian named Cangjie invented the Chinese writing system. According to stories, he had four eyes and could see things others could not. He's said to have found the idea for writing from studying nature, including animals' and birds' tracks and claw marks in the ground. The system for entering Chinese characters into a computer is named for him.

There have been multiple Chinese scripts over the years. The major script types still used today are seal script, clerical or official script, cursive script, semi-cursive or running script, and standard or regular script.

Understanding the type of script used in a piece of calligraphy can be important to understanding the art form and individual pieces of art.

This bronze relief of Cangjie is on the John Adams Building of the Library of Congress in Washington, D.C.

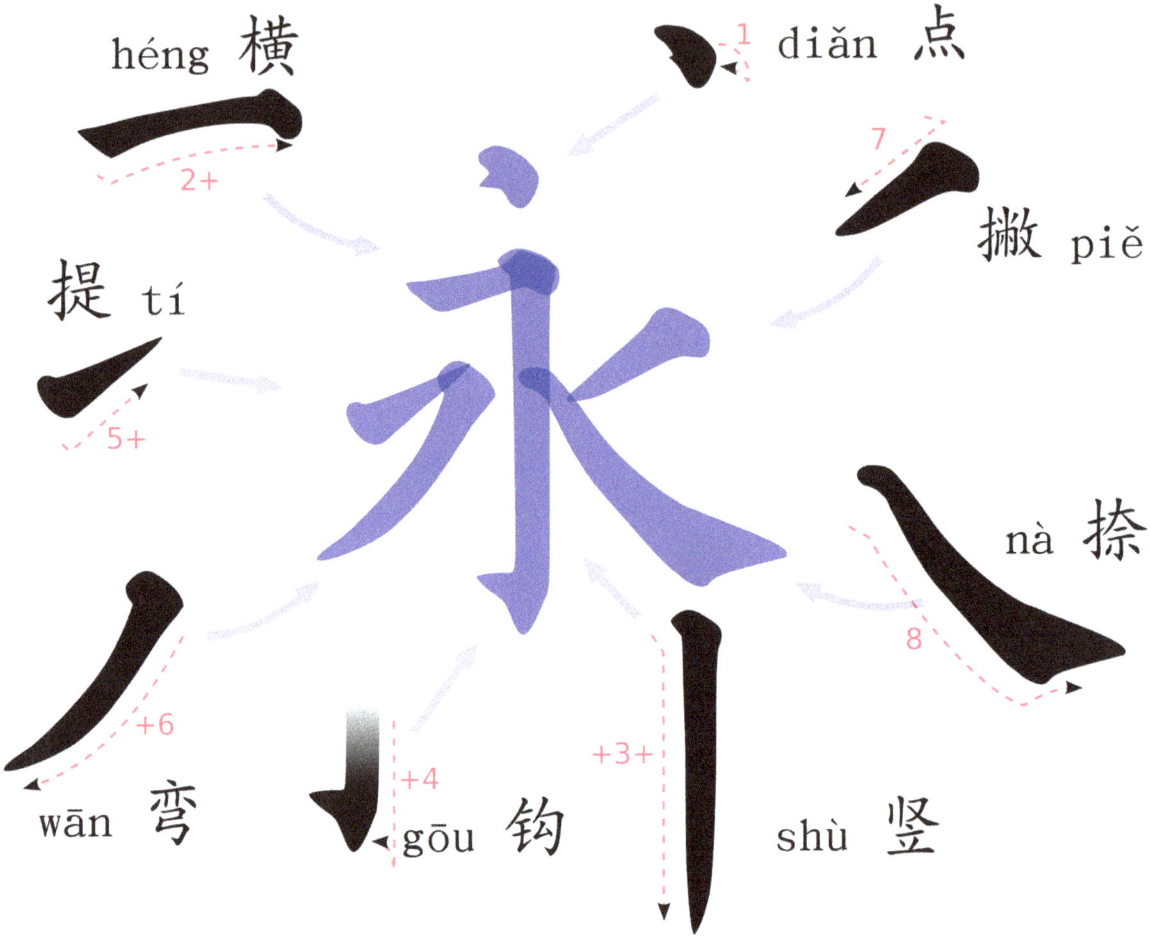

This diagram uses the character *yǒng* ("forever" or "eternal") to show each of the eight main strokes.

Chinese writing is one of the oldest systems of writing in continuous use as a living language, or one that's still commonly used. Egyptian hieroglyphs may be older, but they're no longer in use for a living language.

Of the Chinese scripts, seal script is the oldest. Most people today can't read it, but it's still used for calligraphy and seals. In cursive and running scripts, often used for art, characters may flow together and be harder to read. Standard script is the most common and is the first script most Chinese students learn. It's the newest script, but it's also still nearly 2,000 years old! There are more than 50,000 characters, but most people use far fewer.

Chinese characters are made up of many different strokes. These may be classified in different ways, but there are generally eight main forms. These are *diǎn* (dot), *héng* (horizontal), *shù* (vertical), *piě* (throw away, or left-slanting downward), *nà* (press down, or right-slanting downward), *tí* (rise, or upward lifting), *wān* (bend or curve), and *gōu* (hook). They must be written in a certain order and according to certain rules for each character.

Revered Artists

There have been many honored calligraphers who've greatly promoted the art over the centuries in China. Many were also painters, but some artists are more well known for their calligraphy. Wang Xizhi and his son Wang Xianzhi, who lived in the fourth century CE, were two of the greatest. Not many of their original works have survived to today, but many students copied their works and their style, particularly that of Wang Xizhi.

> Emperor Taizong of the Tang Dynasty was a big fan of Wang Xizhi's work. In fact, he collected hundreds of pieces of it. There's even a story that Taizong sent a court official to get the original of the *Lantingxu*. The story says the official was eventually successful, and after Taizong died, the work was buried with him.

Perhaps Wang Xizhi's most famous work—and perhaps the most famous work of Chinese calligraphy ever—is the *Lantingxu*, or *Preface to the Poems Composed at the Orchid Pavilion*. It's written in running script and relates a gathering of many literary figures (including Wang Xizhi) to drink wine and compose poems in 353 CE. Another famous work is the ***Ritual** to Pray for Good Harvest.*

This portrait of Wang Xizhi is shown with a copy of the *Lantingxu*. There are many copies and some engravings of the work.

Chairman Mao Zedong was himself a calligrapher. Many images showed him working with a brush, and his work is still widely displayed. People copy his calligraphy style, and his handwriting is commonly recognized.

Of course, there have been many other famous and prominent Chinese calligraphers through the years. Some, including Zhao Mengfu, Wen Zhengming, and Dong Qichang, were also well known as painters. Others famous calligraphers include Ouyang Xun and Yan Zhenqing of the Tang Dynasty and Su Shi and Mi Fu of the Song Dynasty.

Of course, people still practice Chinese calligraphy in modern times. It's no longer key to being considered part of elite society, but it is still a beautiful and respected form of art. One prominent modern calligrapher is Wang Dongling, who was born in 1945. He's the director of the Modern Calligraphy Research Center at the China Academy of Art, and his work has been displayed all over the world.

Rules and Related Forms

There can be a lot of flexibility to Chinese calligraphy, but there are established modern rules to follow—at least according to some calligraphers. Characters must be written with the right strokes and the right stroke order. They must be readable to anyone familiar with the script used. There is flexibility in the kinds of tools used and the way of holding the brush, but the finished product should be neat and precise. However, that said, some more modern artists definitely do their own thing in regard to these rules!

There are also digital styles of Chinese characters, and people can type them on a computer, smartphone, or other device without knowing how to write them by hand. This is convenient, but it has led to something called character blindness, in which people forget how to write them, even if they once knew how.

Today, some artists write Chinese characters with a fountain pen or even brush pens or pencils. You can write with ballpoint pens, but it can be difficult to correctly form the thickness of the lines. Gel pens or felt-tip pens may work a bit better.

People can and often do write Chinese characters with a pen. It just won't be calligraphic art!

"Pinyin" refers to a system used to write the words of Modern Standard Chinese (based on Mandarin) in the Latin alphabet. Children learn the Latin alphabet too and then the Pinyin words as well as Chinese characters. There's a lot to learn!

In recent years, the practice of water calligraphy has become popular, particularly with older, often retired, Chinese people. In this hobby, people use long brushes to write large Chinese characters on the pavement, often in parks and other public areas. They use water rather than ink, and the characters evaporate within a relatively brief span of time.

Some people use water calligraphy as part of a connection to Buddhism, a meditation on the concept of impermanence. Others use it as an artistic outlet, to promote the Chinese written language, or just to have fun. It can also be a sort of performance art. Some water calligraphers use special brushes with sponge tips to create their work.

Water calligraphy started in Beijing and then spread. You can now find multiple people practicing it in public parks throughout the country.

The Traditions Continue

Chinese art—including painting and calligraphy—is part of continuous traditions stretching back thousands of years, intertwined with Chinese history itself. Painting and calligraphy are only two of the many forms of art in the region. Other visual arts also have thriving traditions. These include sculpture, pottery, architecture, textiles, and more. And, of course, there are also wealthy legacies of music and literature.

History relates the names of relatively few female painters or calligraphers in ancient, imperial, or early modern China. Some notable ones, however, are Guan Daosheng of the Yuan Dynasty, Qiu Zhu of the Ming Dynasty, and Chen Shu of the Qing Dynasty. In more recent years, Chen Peiqiu (1923–2020) has been called the foremost female Chinese painter of her time.

However, there may be no more intrinsically Chinese art than calligraphy, the art of the line, and the painting that's so connected to it. With such simple tools such as a brush, ink, water, and paper or silk, an artist can create works to awe, to inspire, and make people think. From Gu Kaizhi to Chen Shaoqiang and Wang Dongling, many people have worked to bring such beauty to life. More female artists are also getting a chance to step into the spotlight.

The National Art Museum of China in Beijing is the only national art museum in the country.

Glossary

criticize To judge or find fault with someone or something.

dialect A form of language spoken in a certain area that uses some of its own words, grammar, and pronunciations.

dynasty A family of rulers who control a country for a long time, or the time during a dynasty's rule.

heritage The traditions and beliefs that are a part of the history of a group or nation.

influence An effect one thing has on another.

intricate Having many parts.

legend A story coming down from the past that is popularly accepted but can't be checked.

Mongol A member of an ethnic group native to an area in and around Mongolia in East Asia.

mural A large picture painted on a wall.

Neolithic A time period of the late Stone Age, between the Paleolithic period and the Bronze Age.

philosophy The study of the basic ideas about knowledge, right and wrong, reasoning, and the value of things.

prominent Widely and popularly known.

ritual Having to do with rites or a ritual, or an established form of a ceremony.

scholar A learned person, a person who studies at a school.

script A style of written characters.

technique A method of accomplishing a task.

tradition A way of thinking, behaving, or doing something that's been used by people in a particular society for a long time.

UNESCO The United Nations Educational, Scientific, and Cultural Organization.

For More Information

China Academy of Art
Various campuses
Hangzhou, Zhejiang Province, China
Website: en.caa.edu.cn/
This public fine arts college was established in 1928. It includes a school for painting and calligraphy and many research institutes focusing on subjects including these art forms.

The National Art Museum of China
1 Wusi Ave., Dongcheng District
Beijing, China
Website: www.namoc.org/en/
This art museum, opened in 1963, is China's biggest. It's open to the public free of charge and includes many different forms of art.

National Museum of China
16 Chang'an Ave.
Dongcheng District, China
+86 10 6511 6400
Website: en.chnmuseum.cn
The National Museum of China is the second most-visited museum in the world. It holds many artifacts related to the country and the region, including many works of calligraphy and painting.

Princeton University Art Museum
Elm Drive
Princeton, New Jersey
(609) 258-3788
Website: artmuseum.princeton.edu/
This museum collection of Chinese calligraphy is often considered one of the finest outside Asia.

Smithsonian National Museum of Asian Art
1050 Independence Ave., SW
Washington, DC
(202) 633-1000
Website: asia.si.edu/
This museum is part of the Smithsonian in the United States, and includes a great deal of art from China as well as many other Asian countries.

UNESCO Headquarters
7, place de Fontenoy, 75007
Paris, France
+33 (0) 1 45 68 10 00
Website: en.unesco.org
UNESCO is the United Nations Educational, Scientific, and Cultural Organization. Among other things, it maintains a list of World Heritage sites.

For Further Reading

Captivating History. *Ancient China.* Independently published: Captivating History, 2019.

Kunfeng Huang. *Illustrated Guide to 50 Masterpieces of Chinese Paintings*. New York, NY: Better Link Press, 2019.

Ni, Mike. *Simplified Chinese for Beginners*. Independently published, 2021.

Ruo Mei. *Chinese Brush Painting: A Beginner's Step-by-Step Guide.* New York, NY, and Shanghai, China: Shanghai Press, 2018.

Self, Caroline, and Self, Susan. *A Beginner's Guide to Chinese Brush Painting: 35 Painting Activities from Calligraphy to Animals and Landscapes*. Toyko, Japan: Toyko Publishing, 2021.

Yat-Ming Cathy Ho. *The Art of Chinese Calligraphy*. New York, NY: Chartwell Books, 2016.

Bibliography

"Chinese Calligraphy: An Introduction." Khan Academy. www.khanacademy.org/humanities/art-asia/imperial-china/beginners-guide-imperial-china/a/chinese-calligraphy-an-introduction

"Cultural Sources of Chinese Calligraphy: The Connection of Chinese Calligraphy and Brush Painting." Asian Brushpainter. www.asianbrushpainter.com/blogs/kb/the-connection-of-chinese-calligraphy-and-brush-painting

"Chinese Scholar's Study." Minneapolis Museum of Art. new.artsmia.org/programs/teachers-and-students/teaching-the-arts/artwork-in-focus/chinese-scholars-study

"Chinese Painting." Embassy of the People's Republic of China in the Republic of Malta. January 11, 2017. mt.china-embassy.gov.cn/eng/zgly/201701/t20170113_9826950.htm

"Zuojiang Huashan Rock Art Cultural Landscape." UNESCO World Heritage Convention. whc.unesco.org/en/list/1508/

Richman-Abdou, Kelly. "The Exquisite Artistry and History of Chinese Silk Painting." My Modern Met. March 1, 2020. mymodernmet.com/silk-painting-history/

"Asian Art Collection: China Timeline." Princeton University Art Museum. 2023. static.artmuseum.princeton.edu/asian-art/china/timeline

"Chinese Painting." China Online Museum. www.comuseum.com/painting/

"Chinese Calligraphy." China Online Museum. www.comuseum.com/calligraphy/

"Night-Shining White." The Metropolitan Museum of Art. www.metmuseum.org/art/collection/search/39901

"Chinese Calligraphy." Asia Society. asiasociety.org/education/chinese-calligraphy

"Chinese Language: Myths and Facts." Asia Society. asiasociety.org/education/chinese-language

"An Introduction to Chinese Calligraphy." Christie's. May 14, 2023. www.christies.com/en/stories/expert-guide-to-chinese-calligraphy

Index